TRAVELS SWEET ZOMBIE HORSE
`TO THE BLUE PLANET`

By Dr Phil Freizinger

© Copyright – Phil Fryer – 2023

It is not legal to reproduce, duplicate, or transmit any part of this document in either electronic means or printed format. Recording of this publication is strictly prohibited.

2

`BULLABURRA`

The Sweet Zombie Horse slowly opens her eyes

Below the blue planet-What a sumptuous surprise!

`Let's go-Neigh Neigh Neigh-My wings open wide

To the boomerang land -To the kangaroos` side`

4

`SHIP OF DANGER`

To the skies once again-high above the waves

The golden ship sailing with Pirates so brave

`Let's laugh with the crew as they journey so far

our voices sing `ra pa pa and a ra pa pa``

6

`SWEET ZOMBIE HORSE`

`Who am I?` She neighed,
`Where do I hide?`

`Who am I?` She neighed
`Where do I ride?`

`I`m the Sweet Zombie Horse with a magical mane

and a flying tail that never ends`

`FIESTA D`AMOR`

To Mexico where the hot chillis grow

Will the Mariachis wear the sombrero?

The dancers move with a timeless grace

So fast to the sound of the castanets

`BLUE SKIES SUNSHINE`

Now to the fields of Glastonbury Fest

The rain is streaming- the mud is a mess

`With Magic I scream an equine whine

To make Blue Skies and Summer Sunshine.`

`BANGRA BEAT`

Like lightning to the Ganges and Katmandu

To Dacca -To Nepal -and Mount Everest too

Below she espied with her Equine Eyes

The Bangra dancing -`What a sumptuous surprise!`

Now her journey rides to an end

The Sweet Zombie Horse is always your friend

Wave goodbye as she neighs beyond the skies

Will you meet her again for an equine Surprise?

ABOUT THE SWEET ZOMBIE HORSE

Little is known about the origins of `The Sweet Zombie Horse.`What we do know is that she is a magical being that moves effortlessly between universes and dimensions.

When asked where she comes from, she will simply say `Neigh and Neigh!` Maybe she doesn't know the answer to this question herself or perhaps she thinks the question itself is meaningless.

Her playful nature and sense of humor are the stuff of legends. This makes her the perfect travelling companion for adventurous children. Remember when it comes to The Sweet Zombie Horse the `tail` never ends.

Dedication

In memory of Margaret Fryer, my mum - a teacher in Oxford UK, who shared the joy of reading with so many children for over 30 years

And a special thanks to my partner and musical co-spirit, Sue Smith, our daughter Ella and Renzo, our Grandson, for the inspiration for `The Sweet Zombie Horse`

Neigh! Neigh!

Acknowledgements

To my family and friends who supported me in this exciting new project.
Love and Music to all.

A big thanks to Peter, Emily and the art work team for all their hard work, commitment and skill in bringing 'The Sweet Zombie Horse` to life in the first 3 books.

About the Author

Dr Phil Freizinger has been a professional musician since 1991 playing solo as the flautist `Freizinger` and in many ensembles including `Aquabats` and `The Mighty Redox` which he founded with his partner Sue Smith in the late 90`s.

He has a PhD in Philosophy from The University of Warwick 1980 and a Music Degree from the Birmingham Conservatoire 1993 UK.

He is the writer of many songs and stories which paved the way for his current writing `Travels with the Sweet Zombie Horse`. The stories were inspired by the song Phil and his then 6 year old Grandson, Renzo, wrote in lockdown. `Neigh! Neigh!`

CREDITS

WRITTEN AND NARRATED BY
DR PHIL FREIZINGER

MUSIC BY
THE MIGHTY REDOX

RECORDED BY
NICK MOORBATH AT EVOLUTION STUDIO OXFORD UK

MASTERED BY
TIM TURAN AT TURAN AUDIO OXFORD UK

AND SPECIAL THANKS TO
JOSHUA SQUASHUA FOR THE ORIGINAL AND INSPIRATIONAL ZOMBIE HORSE GRAPHIC.

21

THE END

22

Milton Keynes UK
Ingram Content Group UK Ltd.
UKHW020612251123
433183UK00010B/89